CRISTIANO RONALDO

SOCCER CHAMPION

JASON PORTERFIELD

Britannica
Educational Publishing

IN ASSOCIATION WITH

ROSEN
EDUCATIONAL SERVICES

Published in 2019 by Britannica Educational Publishing (a trademark of Encyclopædia Britannica, Inc.) in association with The Rosen Publishing Group, Inc.
29 East 21st Street, New York, NY 10010

Distributed exclusively by Rosen Publishing.
To see additional Britannica Educational Publishing titles, go to rosenpublishing.com.

First Edition

Britannica Educational Publishing
J. E. Luebering: Executive Director, Core Editorial
Andrea R. Field: Managing Editor, Compton's by Britannica

Rosen Publishing
Kathy Kuhtz Campbell: Senior Editor
Nelson Sá: Art Director
Nicole Russo-Duca: Series Designer and Book Layout
Cindy Reiman: Photography Manager
Sherri Jackson: Photo Researcher

Library of Congress Cataloging-in-Publication Data

Names: Porterfield, Jason, author.
Title: Cristiano Ronaldo: soccer champion / Jason Porterfield.
Description: New York: Britannica Educational Publishing, in Association with Rosen Educational Services, 2019. | Series: Living legends of sports | Includes bibliographical references and index. | Audience: Grades 5–8.
Identifiers: LCCN 2017048733| ISBN 9781538302170 (library bound) | ISBN 9781538302187 (pbk.)
Subjects: LCSH: Ronaldo, Cristiano, 1985– —Juvenile literature. | Soccer players—Portugal—Biography—Juvenile literature.
Classification: LCC GV942.7.R626 P67 2019 | DDC 796.334092 [B] —dc23
LC record available at https://lccn.loc.gov/2017048733

Manufactured in the United States of America

CONTENTS

INTRO-DUCTION

The first half of the 2016–17 Champions League title game between Spain's Real Madrid and Italy's Juventus was close. Juventus came out with a defense that was heavy on the right side to counter Real Madrid's superstar player, Cristiano Ronaldo.

The strategy didn't work, and Ronaldo scored the first goal of the match after about 20 minutes. The teams were tied as the second half began. Then Madrid pulled ahead with two quick scores. For the third goal, Ronaldo slipped past star defender Leonardo Bonucci and angled the ball past the diving goalkeeper, Gianluigi Buffon. Real Madrid went on to win the game 4–1.

In a flash, Ronaldo had shown the world that his speed and footwork could beat two of the world's best defenders. It was a typical display of talent by Ronaldo. His soccer skills have taken him from his humble upbringing in Portugal to international superstardom in Great Britain and Spain. He has played against and beaten some of the best players to ever walk onto the field.

Though he has always been skilled, Ronaldo made himself an even better player through hard work. He quickly learned from other players and applied his talent to become one of the world's leading scorers. He has left a lasting mark on the sport that made him famous.

Real Madrid star Cristiano Ronaldo shoots over Juventus goalkeeper Gianluigi Buffon to score a goal during the Champions League final on June 3, 2017.

ONE

A Champion Grows Up

Cristiano Ronaldo dos Santos Aveiro was born on February 5, 1985, in the town of Funchal, on the small island of Madeira, Portugal. His father, José Diniz Aveiro, worked as an equipment manager for a local soccer team called Andorinha and as a city gardener. His mother, Maria Dolores dos Santos Aveiro, worked as a cook. Cristiano was the youngest of four children, following his brother, Hugo, and sisters, Elma and Liliana Catia.

The Aveiro family did not have a lot of money. They lived in a very small apartment. Cristiano shared a room with his three older siblings. The children did not have toys and shared the few possessions they owned. Their mother was very religious, and the children were raised as devout Roman Catholics.

QUICK FACT

The name Ronaldo was given to Cristiano in honor of his father's favorite movie actor, Ronald Reagan, who was US president at the time of Cristiano's birth.

Ronaldo was born in the city of Funchal on the southern coast of the Portuguese island of Madeira.

Finding Soccer

Soccer was a popular pastime on Madeira. Many of the people who lived on the island were poor. Soccer was a sport that did not cost much money to play and that brought people together. Anyone could join games or watch from the sidelines.

While still a boy, Cristiano began playing soccer for the small club CF Andorinha. His speed and talent were first recognized during those early games.

Cristiano started playing soccer at an early age. He and other children played games anywhere they could find space. Many of these soccer games took place in alleys. At age eight or nine, Cristiano joined Andorinha, the team for which his father worked. He started out as a right-winger, meaning he played mainly along the sideline on the right side of the field.

Even in the informal alley games he played with his friends, Cristiano took the sport seriously. He wanted to win every match. Sometimes his team would lose and he would cry from disappointment. The other children nicknamed him "crybaby." The cruel nickname did not stop him from playing with passion. Cristiano wanted to win more than ever.

Like many of the other kids on the island, he looked up to professional soccer players. His favorite player was the Portuguese midfielder Luis Figo, who was also his mother's favorite player. Figo played in Portugal for Sporting

Portuguese soccer star Luis Figo (*right*), seen here playing for Barcelona, was young Cristiano's favorite player. During his professional career, Figo also played for Real Madrid, Sporting CP, and Inter Milan.

CP and in Spain for Barcelona and Real Madrid.

Cristiano was often one of the smaller players on the field, but his quickness and agility helped him stand out. At age 10, he began playing for Clube Desportivo Nacional of Madeira, the island's biggest team. It was clear even then that he had exceptional talent.

Professional clubs outside Madeira began sending scouts to watch Cristiano play. They believed his competitive spirit and his athleticism would help him become an even better player. They wanted him to play for their clubs.

At age 12, Cristiano transferred to Sporting Clube de Portugal (known as Sporting CP). Sporting CP is a professional team, meaning that its athletes are paid to play soccer. Cristiano could begin making money as a professional athlete playing the

QUICK FACT

Sporting CP was one of the founding clubs of Portugal's Primeira Liga (Premier League) in 1934.

Cristiano (*left*) honed his skills while playing for Sporting CP's youth teams in games like this one against the Wolverhampton Wanderers on July 18, 2002.

sport he loved. He moved to Lisbon, the Portuguese capital, and began playing for Sporting CP's youth teams.

Early Turmoil

Cristiano's passion for succeeding at soccer did not cross over to all other parts of his life. He was uninterested in school when he was a child. Often, Cristiano skipped homework assignments to play soccer. He even sneaked out of his room to play when he was supposed to be working or studying.

Cristiano also had problems at school. He was known for his competitive nature and his fiery temper. When he was 14, he was kicked out of school for throwing a chair at a teacher. He has said that the teacher had disrespected him. His mother decided that the best way to keep him out of trouble was to have him concentrate on playing soccer.

When Cristiano was 15, he was diagnosed with a rapid heartbeat. His heart would race when he was sitting still. The heart condition was one that could cause problems for him as he aged. He could even have a heart attack while he was playing soccer. Cristiano had an operation to fix his heart problem. Doctors used a laser to fix the part of his heart that was causing the problem. He recovered quickly and was back on the field within a few days.

Ronaldo (*right*), playing for Sporting CP, tries to block a shot by FC Porto's Derlei during a match on June 1, 2003.

The Next Level

Cristiano used his time in Sporting CP's youth leagues to improve his skills. He practiced his footwork to become a better ball handler. He also began working out with weights. He wanted to be big enough and strong enough to play with the professionals on Sporting CP's first (top-level) team.

QUICK FACT

Cristiano was only 17 years old when he moved up to Sporting CP's first team.

Cristiano's chance to prove himself on the first team came during the 2002–03 season. He had earned the opportunity with his speed, quickness, and ball-handling skills. He had also grown taller. His new height, 6 feet and 1 inch, made him better suited to play as a forward from the right wing. He scored his first professional goal for Sporting CP on October 7, 2002.

CHAPTER TWO

Developing Skills

Cristiano Ronaldo was already well known across Portugal in 2003. He was one of the biggest stars on Sporting CP. His youth and skills made him an exciting player to watch. He was expected to play mostly as a backup to the more experienced players on the team, but his skills led him to play more and more.

The Move to Manchester

On August 6, 2003, the acclaimed British soccer team Manchester United came to Portugal to play a friendly. This is a game between two professional teams from different leagues that does not count in the standings in either league. Manchester United had been touring the United States and won four games against teams there before arriving in Portugal. The friendly celebrated the opening of Sporting CP's new soccer stadium, Estádio José Alvalade.

Sporting CP beat Manchester United easily by a score of 3–1. Ronaldo did not score any goals during the game, but he outplayed Manchester United fullback John O'Shea. Ronaldo kept O'Shea working so hard that the older man had to see a doctor at halftime because he was having dizzy spells.

Lisbon's Estádio José Alvalade is Sporting CP's home stadium. It also hosted five games of the European Championship tournament in 2004.

The match gave Sporting CP a win in the new stadium. It also gave Manchester United coach Sir Alex Ferguson a firsthand look at Ronaldo's playing abilities. Ferguson thought that Ronaldo would fit in well as a Manchester United player. He liked Ronaldo's speed and agility. Manchester United, a member of the Premier League, was one of the most famous soccer teams in the world. The team had recently lost its biggest star, David Beckham, who had left to play for Real Madrid in Spain at the end of the 2002–03 season.

Just days after the friendly, Manchester United offered Ronaldo a contract. It would give him the chance to play for a team that was recognized by fans all over the globe. It would also mean having to leave Portugal and the world he knew. Ronaldo chose to sign the contract. In a flash, he became one of the richest athletes in soccer.

Manchester United coach Sir Alex Ferguson (*left*) welcomed Cristiano Ronaldo to the club after Ronaldo signed a contract in Manchester, England, on August 12, 2003.

QUICK FACT

Eighteen-year-old Ronaldo's £12.2-million ($19.5-million) contract was the largest ever given to such a young player.

Ronaldo took his family to England to live with him. He bought a house and told his mother that she would never have to work again. He wanted them to share in his good fortune.

Coach Ferguson moved carefully to make sure Ronaldo became used to the Premier League's style of play. He decided that Ronaldo would start his first season on the bench and would be eased into games later. This option would give Ronaldo some playing time against Premier League athletes without putting too much pressure on him.

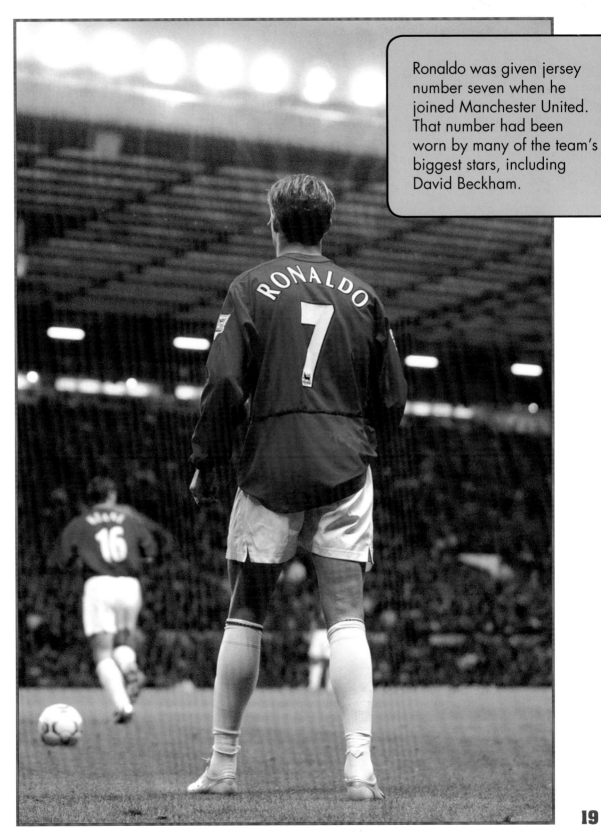

Ronaldo was given jersey number seven when he joined Manchester United. That number had been worn by many of the team's biggest stars, including David Beckham.

The first chance to put Ronaldo in a game came on the Premier League's opening day, August 16, 2003. Ronaldo came off the bench as a late-game substitute against the Bolton Wanderers. He played for 30 minutes in a game that Manchester United won by a score of 4–0. During the game, he beat multiple defenders with his speed and footwork, drawing a penalty and making a perfect free kick. It looked like Coach Ferguson had been right about Ronaldo being a good fit for Manchester United.

Growing on the Field

Ronaldo's first game for Manchester United showed the team and its fans that he could be a great player. He regularly appeared late in games as Coach Ferguson had planned. He scored his first goal for the team on a free kick on November 1, 2003, late in a home game against Portsmouth that Manchester United won 3–0.

The victory was a solid win during an uneven season for the team. Manchester United finished the 2003–04 regular season ranked third in the Premier League standings. The team won its then-record 11th Football Association Challenge Cup (FA Cup) by beating Millwall 3–0. However, Manchester United failed to advance far in the Champions League and League Cup tournaments.

Ronaldo played a part in the FA Cup victory by scoring two goals. The first was in a game against rival club Manchester City. The second was in the final game. He finished the season with a total of six goals in limited playing time.

QUICK FACT

The Premier League is the top division of soccer in England. It is made up of 20 teams.

Ronaldo had supporters and critics in the stands at Manchester. Many fans loved his speed and his ability to score. Others felt that he needed to pass to his teammates more often.

Even when Manchester United's season ended, Ronaldo kept playing. He was a member of Portugal's

Ronaldo's agility and athleticism were on display during his Premier League debut on August 16, 2003. Here he leaps over a tackle by Bolton Wanderers player Bruno N'Gotty.

national team in the European Championship. He led his home country's team to the final match, but Portugal lost the championship to Greece.

Ronaldo quickly became used to the tough and physical style of play in the Premier League. He also matured physically. He entered the league as a very skinny teenager. He began working out more and adding muscle to his frame. He learned how to use his speed to score more goals. Soon, he was considered one of soccer's best forwards.

Ronaldo also became known for his emotional style of play. The

way he played sometimes angered opposing fans. Sometimes, he had outbursts on the field. In 2006, he was banned for a game and fined for making a rude gesture at fans during a Manchester United loss to Benefica during a Champions League game in Portugal. At other times, he fought with opposing players or even with members of his own team. Opposing fans often booed him because they did not like the way he played.

Ronaldo's talent could not be denied. He was a key player for Portugal's national

Ronaldo holds Manchester United's Sir Matt Busby Player of the Year Award, which he received on August 12, 2007. Fans vote for the trophy winner. Ronaldo also won the award in 2004 and 2008.

team in the 2006 World Cup tournament. He led his home country's team to a fourth-place finish, which was far higher than many fans expected.

Playing for Manchester United, he showed himself to be a real scoring threat during the 2006–07 season. The season began poorly for Ronaldo. He was even booed by Manchester United fans during a friendly against Oxford. Some fans believed he was responsible for England player Wayne Rooney taking a red card and being forced to leave England's game against Portugal in the quarterfinals of the 2006 World Cup tournament.

Ronaldo used the booing to motivate him. The 2006–07 season turned out to be his breakout season for Manchester United. He finished the season with 23 total goals, including those he scored in tournament play.

Ronaldo was a major part of the team's finish at the top of the Premier League standings. The title was Manchester United's first since the 2002–03 season. Ronaldo was recognized for his pivotal role in the team's success. At the end of the season, he was named Professional Footballers' Association Player of the Year and Young Player of the Year. Outside the league, he was recognized as the Football Writers' Association Player of the Year.

CHAPTER THREE

Becoming a Champion

Ronaldo had his best season in the Premier League in 2007–08, one that made him a legend in English soccer. He steadily increased his scoring numbers as he received more time on the field. Although he was still a bold and intensely competitive player who sometimes angered fans, he was also becoming a leader on the field.

A Glorious Season

Ronaldo's 2007–08 season for Manchester United was spectacular. His accomplishments that season earned him comparisons to the great Manchester United player George Best.

Ronaldo and Manchester United started slowly. He was sent out of the team's second game of the season with a red card for head-butting a Portsmouth player. The game finished in a 1–1 draw. Ronaldo was banned from playing in the team's next three games.

Ronaldo scores against Wigan Athletic during a Premier League match on October 6, 2007. Manchester United won the match by a score of 4–0.

When he returned from the ban, he began scoring like never before. He scored 31 Premier League goals during 34 league games that season. With Ronaldo providing such strong offense, Manchester United finished first in the league standings. His scoring success extended to Champions League and FA Cup competition. He finished the 2007–08 season with 42 goals across all play.

Manchester United won the Premier League and Champions League titles. Ronaldo scored a key goal in winning the final game of the Champions League tournament against Chelsea.

By the end of the season, Ronaldo was recognized as one of the greatest players in the world. He was awarded the Premier League Golden Boot trophy for being that league's leading scorer. He also earned the Golden Shoe as Europe's leading scorer. The Fédération Internationale de Football Association (FIFA) named him World Player of

Ronaldo was awarded the Golden Shoe as the top scorer across European leagues in 2007–08. It was the first time he won the prize.

2007
2008

the Year for 2008. He was also named the captain of Portugal's national team. All of that success came when he was only 23 years old. Many thought that a player so young and so gifted could only improve.

The 2008–09 season was not as successful as the previous season, but it was still a great year for Ronaldo. He scored 26 goals in 53 games. Ronaldo helped lead Manchester United to the final game of the Champions League tournament. However, the team lost the title to FC Barcelona.

Departing for Spain

Ronaldo had signed a new five-year contract with Manchester United in 2007. Manchester United fans who had watched him grow into a superstar hoped to see him stay with the club until at least 2012. However, his international fame, his youth, and his enormous talent meant that many other teams wanted to sign him.

In 2009, Ronaldo transferred to Real Madrid, in

Real Madrid president Florentino Perez (*left*) looks on as Ronaldo signs a contract to join the renowned Spanish team at Santiago Bernabéu Stadium in 2009.

Spain. Real Madrid, a member of La Liga, has long been one of the world's top soccer teams. There had been rumors that Ronaldo wanted to play for Real Madrid. Signing with a Spanish club would put him and his family closer to his native Portugal.

Ronaldo's contract with Real Madrid was worth £80 million (about $131 million). It set a record for professional soccer players and was more valuable than all but a few professional athletes worldwide.

Continued Excellence

Ronaldo justified his contract with Real Madrid through exceptional play from the beginning of the season. He scored nine goals in his first seven games, helping the team win each of those contests.

Ronaldo scored two of those goals during the seventh game of the season in a 3–0 victory over Champions League opponent Marseille. He also sprained his right ankle. The injury was at first believed to be minor. When he tried to come back from it too early, he reinjured it during a World Cup qualifying match for Portugal. He missed two months of play and nine matches while he recovered.

Ronaldo scored the only goal in the final of the Copa del Rey competition on April 20, 2011. Real Madrid defeated Barcelona 1–0 at Mestalla Stadium in Valencia, Spain.

Ronaldo returned to the field in late November 2009 in a Champions League match against FC Zürich. Real Madrid won that match and played well for the rest of the season. The team finished second in the La Liga standings. Ronaldo finished his first season in Madrid with 33 goals, 26 in La Liga competition and another seven in Champions League games.

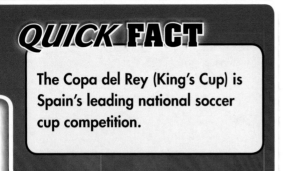

Ronaldo was even better the next season. He avoided injuries and played in 34 league games in 2010–11. He used dazzling footwork to confuse his opponents and bursts of speed to get past them. He finished the season with 40 La Liga goals, setting a league record. He scored an additional 13 goals in tournament play, finishing the season with 53 goals in 54 games. Ronaldo even scored the winning goal in Madrid's victory over Barcelona in the final of the Copa del Rey competition.

La Liga Legend

Ronaldo continued his outstanding play for Real Madrid. He helped the team win the La Liga championship in 2011–12. Ronaldo scored 46 goals in 38 league games that year. He finished the season with 60 total goals for Madrid. In 2012–13, he scored another 55 goals for the team.

Ronaldo's skills and his leadership abilities on the field were obvious to Real Madrid fans. They fully embraced him as their star player. Few other soccer professionals had his ability to instantly change games. He was also recognized globally for his accomplishments. Ronaldo's many stellar achievements led to FIFA awarding him the Ballon d'Or prize (the renamed World Player of the Year award) for 2012–13.

Ronaldo continued to excel. He scored 51 total goals for Real Madrid in 2013–14. He won his third Ballon d'Or prize. Real Madrid finished third in the La Liga standings but won the Copa del Rey. The team beat Barcelona 2–1 in the championship game.

Ronaldo won the 2013 FIFA Ballon d'Or award. Here he poses with the trophy during an awards gala held on January 13, 2014, at the Kongresshaus in Zürich, Switzerland.

Unfortunately, Ronaldo missed that game and the two matches before it because of injuries to his left knee and thigh. Ronaldo struggled with injury for the rest of the season, but he was able to compete in the Champions League final. He scored a goal to help Real Madrid defeat Atlético Madrid for the Champions League title.

Ronaldo won the La Liga season scoring title for 2014–15 by scoring 48 goals in league matches. He finished the season with 61 total goals. In the 2015–16 season, he scored 35 goals in La Liga play while helping Real Madrid win its 11th Champions League title. He was awarded his fourth Ballon d'Or prize for his play that season. Only Lionel Messi had won the award more times.

Playing for Portugal in 2016, Ronaldo took the team all the way through the European Championship tournament. Portugal beat France 1–0 in the final round to claim its first major international trophy.

Ronaldo continued his dominant play in 2016–17. He scored 42 goals that season across all play for Real Madrid. The team won the La Liga and Champions League titles. After the season, Ronaldo was named Best FIFA Men's Player. He also beat out his rivals Lionel Messi and Neymar to win his fifth Ballon d'Or award, tying Messi's record. Even at age 32, Ronaldo showed no signs of slowing down. In 2016, he signed a new contract with Real Madrid, keeping him with the team until 2021.

CHAPTER FOUR

Off the Field

Ronaldo is an international celebrity and one of the world's most recognizable athletes. He has won many of soccer's most desirable awards. His teams have dominated league and international tournaments.

His success has led him to great wealth. He has signed many sponsorship deals with internationally recognized brands. He has lived a glamorous lifestyle in the public eye in England and in Spain. Even though he has been surrounded by luxury and wealth since signing his first contract with Manchester United, Ronaldo has never forgotten the poverty he witnessed while growing up in Madeira. He has since become one of the world's most generous celebrities.

Fashion and Sponsors

Ronaldo has always shown a flair for fashion when not in uniform. Even when he was younger, he tended to attract attention with his clothes. He has since turned his unique taste into a business off the field.

QUICK FACT

Madeira's airport features a bronze bust of Ronaldo. To honor the soccer superstar, the airport was renamed Cristiano Ronaldo International Airport in March 2017.

Fashion and design are very important to Ronaldo when he's off the field. Here he poses in Shanghai, China, with one of his CR7 brand soccer spikes.

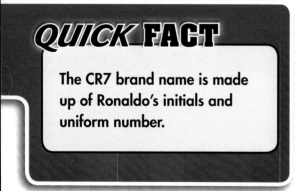

QUICK FACT

The CR7 brand name is made up of Ronaldo's initials and uniform number.

Ronaldo launched his own CR7 line of products in 2013. The brand includes athletic clothing and fashion apparel such as dress shirts and shoes. Ronaldo models his own clothes for the brand.

Ronaldo also helps sell products for other brands. He has been a representative for the footwear and sportswear brand Nike for years. In 2016, he became the third athlete ever to have a lifetime endorsement deal with Nike. The other

two people with such deals are National Basketball Association (NBA) superstars Michael Jordan and LeBron James. The deal means that Ronaldo is the face of Nike's soccer gear. Ronaldo's Nike contract, together with his salary, has made him one of the world's richest athletes.

Ronaldo's fame throughout the world helped lead to his sponsorship contract with Nike. He is the first soccer player to receive a lifetime deal with the company.

Family Life

Off the soccer field, Ronaldo places a great deal of importance on his family. His own father was not around much when he was young, so he tries to be there for his children. His first son, Cristiano Ronaldo Jr., was born in 2010. He lives with Ronaldo in Madrid. His twins, Eva and Matteo, were born in June 2017. His fourth child, Alana, followed later

Ronaldo and his oldest child, Cristiano Ronaldo Jr., pose on the red carpet at the 2015 world premiere of the film *Ronaldo* in London. The film tells the story of the soccer star's life.

that year. Ronaldo's mother, Dolores, lives with him in Madrid. He is also close to his sisters and his brother.

In 2013, Ronaldo opened a museum to tell his story and store his memorabilia at the suggestion of his brother, Hugo. Museu CR7 houses his collection of more than 160 trophies and is located in Funchal. A statue of Ronaldo stands in front of the museum. Ronaldo also owns a hotel next door called the Pestana CR7 Hotel.

QUICK FACT

After his father died in 2005 after struggling with alcoholism, Ronaldo campaigned against alcohol and drug abuse.

Museu CR7 is dedicated to telling the story of Ronaldo's life as a professional soccer player. Here Ronaldo stands in street clothes next to a lifelike statue of himself at the museum's opening.

Ronaldo and two other Real Madrid players present children with Christmas gifts at a charity event at the club's stadium.

A Giving Heart

Ronaldo is one of the most charitable celebrities in the world. He has frequently donated to worthy causes and responded generously to major disasters. The website Dosomething.org named Ronaldo the world's most charitable athlete of 2015.

At times, Ronaldo has shown his generosity on a personal level. In 2012, he paid for a nine-year-old boy's cancer treatments after learning that the child was a fan. In 2014, he gave $83,000 to the family of a 10-month-old boy who needed brain surgery. He has visited other sick children in hospitals and has worked to raise awareness of the need for people to become blood donors in Portugal and in Spain.

Ronaldo gave money to help pay for a cancer center in Portugal. The donation had a personal connection for Ronaldo. His mother was treated for breast cancer after being diagnosed with the disease in 2007. Two years later, he donated more than $165,000 to fund the center at the hospital where she was treated.

Ronaldo has supported a wide range of global charities, including Save the Children, World Vision, and UNICEF. Many of his charitable efforts focus on children and people in poverty-stricken places. As early as 2004, when he was just becoming a star, he helped raise money to assist victims of a massive tsunami in the Indian Ocean. He raised money for earthquake victims in Nepal in 2015 and for refugees from the war in Syria. In 2016, he donated his entire Champions League win bonus of €600,000 (about $700,000) to charity.

Ronaldo's generosity and his charitable work have added to his legacy as a living legend of soccer. His efforts on the field have inspired millions of fans worldwide. He will certainly be remembered as one of the great players of his era.

TIMELINE

1985: Cristiano Ronaldo dos Santos Aveiro is born on February 5 in Funchal on the island of Madeira, Portugal.

1997: Cristiano joins Sporting Clube de Portugal (Sporting CP) and begins playing for its youth teams.

1999: Cristiano is expelled from school at age 14 following an angry outburst.

2002: Cristiano makes his debut on Sporting CP's first team at age 17.

2003: Ronaldo signs his first contract with Manchester United. On August 16, he plays in his first game for the team, entering as a substitute.

2005: Ronaldo's father dies after years of alcohol abuse.

2006: Playing for his home country, Ronaldo leads Portugal to a fourth-place finish in the World Cup tournament.

2007: Manchester United wins the team's first Premier League title since 2003. Ronaldo is named the Football Writers' Association Player of the Year.

2008: FIFA names Ronaldo World Player of the Year for 2008.

2009: Ronaldo signs a contract to play for Real Madrid in Spain.

2010: Ronaldo's first child, Cristiano Ronaldo Jr., is born.

2011: Ronaldo scores the winning goal in Real Madrid's Copa del Rey tournament victory.

2012: Ronaldo leads Real Madrid to the La Liga championship.

2013: FIFA awards Ronaldo his second Ballon d'Or. Ronaldo opens his Museu CR7 museum in Funchal to store and display his memorabilia.

2014: FIFA gives Ronaldo his third Ballon d'Or award.

2015: The website Dosomething.org names Ronaldo the world's most charitable athlete.

2016: Ronaldo leads Portugal's national team to its first European Championship. He wins his fourth Ballon d'Or award and signs a new five-year contract with Real Madrid.

2017: Ronaldo is named Best FIFA Men's Player. His twin children, Eva and Matteo, are born in June. His fourth child, Alana, is born in November. In December, Ronaldo wins his fifth Ballon d'Or award, tying Lionel Messi's record of five wins.

Luis Suárez (1987–) led La Liga in scoring in 2015–16 with 40 goals for Barcelona, the most ever by a league player other than Ronaldo and Lionel Messi. He scored his 300th career goal in 2015 and has won two Golden Shoe awards and one Golden Boot award.

Lionel Messi (1987–) has been one of La Liga's most dominant scorers since 2004. He became Barcelona's career leader in goals in 2012 with the 233rd goal of his career. He has won the Ballon d'Or award five times and the Golden Shoe award four times.

Robert Lewandowski (1988–) is a striker for Bayern Munich in the German league Bundesliga. He led the league in scoring twice, in 2013–14 and 2015–16. He was named Polish Footballer of the Year for six years in a row, from 2011 to 2016.

Gareth Bale (1989–) stars alongside Ronaldo for Real Madrid. Bale was named the Professional Footballers' Association Player of the Year in 2011 and 2013. Bale also plays for the Welsh national team and is its second-leading career scorer.

Antoine Griezmann (1991–) led Atlético Madrid to the Champions League final in 2015–16. He scored 32 goals that season, including 22 in La Liga and seven in the Champions League. He was named French Player of the Year and the La Liga Best Player in 2016.

Neymar (1992–) helped Barcelona win La Liga, Copa del Rey, and Champions League trophies in 2014–15. He has also scored more than 50 goals for the Brazilian national team. He scored the winning goal for Brazil in the gold medal match in the 2016 Olympics.

GLOSSARY

agility The ability to move quickly and easily.

athleticism The ability to play sports or do physical activities well.

charitable Freely giving money, food, or other kinds of help to needy or sick people.

competitive Having a strong desire to win or be the best at something.

defender A player in a sport assigned to a defensive position.

diagnose To recognize a disease, illness, or condition by examining someone.

dominate To be much more successful or powerful than others in a game or competition.

endorsement The act of publicly or officially saying that you support or approve of someone or something.

footwork The movement of the feet in a sport or dance.

forward A player who plays near the opponent's goal.

free kick A kick that is made without being stopped or slowed by an opponent and that is allowed because of a foul (an action that is against the rules) by an opponent.

friendly A game between sports teams that has no connection with league or championship play.

fullback A player who is usually positioned near the defensive goal in soccer or various other games.

goalkeeper A player who defends the goal in soccer or various other games.

informal Having a friendly and relaxed quality.

league A group of sports teams that play against each other.

offense The group of players on a team who try to score points against an opponent.

penalty A punishment or disadvantage given to a team or player for breaking a rule in a game.

red card A penalty card given to a player who has received two yellow caution cards in a game and who is ejected from that game.

sidelines The space outside the area where a game is played on a field or court.

sprain To injure a joint by twisting it in a sudden and painful way.

substitute A player who takes the place of another player during a game.

tournament A sports competition consisting of a series of games and involving a number of teams.

tsunami A large wave in the ocean that is usually caused by an underwater earthquake or volcanic eruption and that can cause great destruction when it reaches land.

Books

Burshtein, Karen. *Lionel Messi: Soccer's Top Scorer*. New York, NY: Britannica Educational Publishing, 2016.

Caioli, Luca. *Messi, Neymar, Ronaldo*. Updated ed. New York, NY: Icon Books, 2017.

Doeden, Matt. *Cristiano Ronaldo*. Minneapolis, MN: Lerner Publications, 2017.

Faulkner, Nicholas, and Josepha Sherman. *Soccer: Girls Rocking It*. New York, NY: Rosen Publishing, 2016.

Guillain, Charlotte. *Portugal*. Chicago, IL: Heinemann Library, 2012.

Jökulsson, Illugi. *Ronaldo*. 2nd ed. New York, NY: Abbeville Press Publishers, 2015.

Jökulsson, Illugi. *Stars of World Soccer*. New York, NY: Abbeville Press Publishers, 2015.

Karpovich, Todd. *Manchester United*. Minneapolis, MN: SportsZone, 2018.

Kortemeier, Todd. *Real Madrid CF*. Minneapolis, MN: SportsZone, 2018.

Latham, Andrew. *Soccer Smarts for Kids: 60 Skills, Strategies, and Secrets*. Berkeley, CA: Rockridge Press, 2016.

Logothetis, Paul. *Cristiano Ronaldo: International Soccer Star*. Minneapolis, MN: SportsZone, 2016.

Spragg, Iain. *Cristiano Ronaldo: The Ultimate Fan Book*. 3rd ed. London, UK: Carlton Books, 2017.

Websites

Cristiano Ronaldo
http://www.cristianoronaldo.com

Goal.com
http://www.goal.com/en-us/player/cristiano-ronaldo/
h17s3qts1dz1zqjw19jazzkl

Real Madrid
https://www.realmadrid.com/en/football/squad/
cristiano-ronaldo-dos-santos

TransferMarkt
https://www.transfermarkt.co.uk/cristiano-ronaldo/profil/spieler/8198

INDEX